2 PRACTICE TESTS
FOR THE
OLSAT®
GRADE 2
(3rd Grade Entry)
Level C

ISBN: 978-1-948255-65-3

Origins Publications
New York, NY, USA
Email:info@originspublications.com

Origins Publications

Origins Publications help students develop their higher-order thinking skills while also improving their chances of admission into gifted and accelerated-learner programs.

Our goal is to unleash and nurture the genius in every student. We do this by offering educational and test prep materials that are fun, challenging, and provide a sense of accomplishment.

Please contact us with any questions.

info@originspublications.com

Contents

Part 1: Introduction to the OLSAT®

This book offers an overview of the types of questions on the OLSAT® Level C, test-taking strategies to improve performance, and two full-length practice OLSAT® Level C practice tests that students can use to assess their knowledge and practice their test-taking skills.

Who Takes the OLSAT® Level C?

The OLSAT® Level C is often used as an assessment tool or admissions test in 2nd grade for entry into 3rd grade of gifted and talented programs and highly-competitive schools.

The OLSAT® Level C is also used as an assessment tool by teachers to figure out which students would benefit from an accelerated or remedial curriculum

When Does the OLSAT® Take Place?

This depends on the school district you reside in or want to attend. Check with the relevant school/ district to learn more about test dates and the application/ registration process.

OLSAT® Level C Overview

The OLSAT® is designed to measure an individual's ability to reason logically and think abstractly. Specifically, it tests a variety of skills and abilities in students aged between four and 18, including verbal and quantitative skills and spatial reasoning ability.

The OLSAT® consists of two main parts: verbal and nonverbal.

Verbal questions measure a student's ability to gather and manipulate information from language. They also measure a student's ability to comprehend patterns, relationships, and context clues in order to solve a problem.

To answer these questions, a student needs to be able to fully understand what a question is asking, and make inferences based on what she has heard. A student also benefits from a broad vocabulary knowledge. Although a child needs to understand some verbal language for these sections, all answer choices are shown in a picture format.

Non-verbal questions measure a student's ability to reason her way through non-language based scenarios. These questions take a more visual format, and students answer questions based on information and reasoning from pictures rather than as a result of listening to and reasoning from verbal questions asked by a test administrator.

To answer these questions, a student needs to be able to find the relationship between objects in a pattern, to predict what the next level of the pattern will look like, and generalize the rules he discovers.

Length

The OLSAT® Level C test has 60 multiple-choice questions. The approximate timeline for the test is 77 minutes (with breaks).

Format

The test is a black and white picture-based exam, and consists of 30 verbal questions and 30 non-verbal questions.

Part 2: How to Use this Book

The OLSAT® is an important test and the more a student is familiar with the types of questions on the exam, the better she will fare when taking the test.

This book will help your student get used to the format and content of the test so s/he will be adequately prepared and feel confident on test day

Inside this book, you will find

- Overview of each question type on the test and teaching tips to help your child approach each question type strategically and with confidence

- 2 full-length OLSAT® Level C practice tests and answer keys.

Part 3. Test Prep Tips and Strategies

Firstly, and most importantly, commit to make this test preparation process a stress-free one. A student's ability to keep calm and focused in the face of challenge is a quality that will benefit him or her throughout her academic life.

Be prepared for difficul questions from the get-go! There will be a certain percentage of questions that are very challenging for all children. It is key to encourage students to use all strategies available when faced with challenging questions. And remember that a student can get quite a few questions wrong and still do very well on the test.

Before starting the practice test, go through the sample questions and read the general test prep strategies provided at the beginning of the book. They will help you guide your student as he or she progresses through the practice test.

The following strategies may also be useful as you help your child prepare:

Before You Start

- Find a quiet, comfortable spot to work free of distractions.
- Tell your student you will be doing some fun activities, and that this is an opportunity for you to spend some enjoyable time together.
- Tell your student that she or he should listen carefully to what you say.
- Show your student how to perform the simple technique of shading (and erasing) bubbles.

During Prep

- Encourage your student to look at the answer options as the question is read aloud.
- Encourage your student to carefully consider all the answer options before selecting one. Tell her there is only ONE correct answer.
- If your student is stumped by a question, she or he can use the process of elimination. First, encourage your student to eliminate obviously wrong answers to narrow down the answer choices. If your student is still in doubt after using this technique, tell him or her to guess as there are no points deducted for wrong answers.
- If challenged by a question, ask your student to explain why he or she chose a specific answer. If the answer was incorrect, this will help you identify where your student is stumbling. If the answer was correct, asking your child to articulate her reasoning aloud will help reinforce the concept.
- Review all the questions your student answered incorrectly, and explain to your student why the answer is incorrect. Have your student attempt these questions again a few days later to see if he now understands the concept.
- Encourage your student to do her best, but take plenty of study breaks. Start with 10-15 minute sessions. Your student will perform best if she views these activities as enjoyable and engaging, not as exercises to be avoided.

When to Start Preparing?

Every family and student will approach preparation for this test differently. There is no 'right' way to prepare; there is only the best way for a particular child and family. We suggest students, at minimum, take one full-length practice test and spend 6-8 hours doing/reviewing OLSAT® practice questions.

If you have limited time to prepare, spend most energy reviewing areas where your student is encountering the majority of problems.

As they say, knowledge is power! Preparing for the OLSAT® will certainly help your student avoid anxiety and make sure she does not give up too soon when faced with unfamiliar and perplexing questions.

Part 4: Question Types

The OLSAT® Level C is comprised of seven diffe ent question types:

<u>Verbal</u>

>   Following Directions
>   Aural Reasoning
>   Arithmetic Reasoning

<u>Non-Verbal</u>

>   Analogies
>   Classification
>   Series
>   Pattern Matrices

Following Directions

'Following Directions' questions measure a student's ability to listen carefully and choose a representation (figural design or picture) of a description that is read to a student by a test administrator.

*   These questions test a student's knowledge of relational concepts, including distinguishing between and understanding phrases such as "up", "down", "below", "above", "behind" and "next to."

*   These questions test knowledge of sizes, shapes, and numbers.

*   These questions measure a student's understanding of concepts such as neither/nor, and the order of things, such as first, second, third, etc

SAMPLE QUESTION:

Which picture shows a black triangle under a black heart and a white star?

A   B   C   D

Answer: C

Aural Reasoning

'Aural Reasoning' questions assess a student's ability to listen to, understand and visualize a question that is read aloud to him or her. These questions assess listening skills, visual vocabulary, and understanding about the characteristics and functions of things. They also measure the ability to pay close attention to details, and the ability to use logic and inferences to figure out the correct outcome and response.

SAMPLE QUESTION:

On a vacation, Donna, Ross and Caroline sunbathed on the beach. Donna and Caroline wore sunglasses, but Ross used an umbrella to shade him. Which picture shows this?

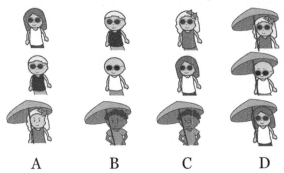

A   B   C   D

Answer: C. This is the only answer where a boy has an umbrella shading him, and two girls are wearing sunglasses.

TIPS: If your student consistently cannot recall all the information read aloud to her in a 'Following Directions' or 'Aural Reasoning' question, leave out some details that are not essential. Gradually add in more information then you think your student is ready. Aim ultimately to read the whole question just once, as this reflects the actual testing environment

Arithmetic Reasoning

The main skill tested by 'Arithmetic Reasoning' questions is the ability to create mathematical problems from language and to solve those problems.

- These questions test a student's ability to listen to verbal directions that require him or her to count objects, contrast quantities, and solve problems that involve addition, subtraction, multiplication and fractions with small numbers.

- Some of these questions assess basic mathematical concepts, while others assess more sophisticated concepts such as reasoning and solving word problems.

TIPS: Try using hands-on materials (like blocks, beads or marbles) to help a student become confident with adding and subtracting. For example, you might give your student two marbles and then ask her to "add" three more marbles to the pile. Then, ask her to count how many marbles she now has. This works with subtraction, too.

Analogies

'Analogies' questions measure a student's ability to reason his or her way through non-language based scenarios.

A student is presented with a 4-box matrix and must identify a relationship between two pictures (or two geometric figures) in the first row. The student needs to apply this rule to the second row an choose which object - from the answer choices - completes this second row relationship in the same way.

The OLSAT® Level C contain two types of analogy questions: picture analogies and figural analogies

Picture Analogies

To master picture analogies, a student needs to have general background knowledge, a good visual vocabulary, and an understanding/recognition of the following relationships:

Part/whole (or reverse: whole/part)
Object/function (or reverse: function/object)
Agent (person or animal)/location, (or reverse: location/agent (person or animal)
Agent (person or animal)/object, (or reverse: object/agent (person or animal)
Agent (person or animal)/action, (or reverse: action/ agent (person or animal)
Change in quantity, size
Familial -- having to do with family.

SAMPLE QUESTION:

Which image best fits in the box with the question mark?

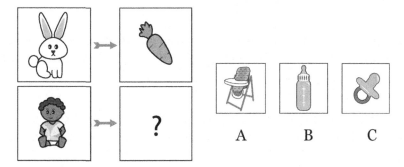

Answer: B. A carrot is food for a rabbit like milk is food for a baby.

Figural Analogies

To succeed on figural analogy questions, student need to understand several key concepts, including geometric concepts such as rotational symmetry, line symmetry, parts of a whole, and opposites.

SAMPLE QUESTION:

Which image best fits in the box with the question mark?

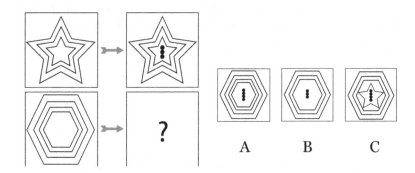

Answer: A. The number of dots in the center of the shape in the top right box is the same as the number of layers of the shape in the top left box. The boxes in the bottom row follow the same rule.

TIPS: On challenging figural questions, a student will have to pay close attention to several aspects of the design (e.g.: color, shape, direction) at the same time. With these questions, encourage your student to isolate one element (e.g.: outer shape, inner shape/s) at a time and identify how it changes.

If your student is challenged by these items, ask specific questions to guide him: Ask: "How do the objects relate to each other in the first row? Do you see a pattern or relationship? "Can you guess what the missing object should be in the second row?" Do you see your prediction in the answer choices?".

Classifications

'Classification' questions assess a student's ability to identify what does not belong among a group of objects (figures or pictures). A student has to evaluate differences and similarities among the items i order to correctly answer the question.

- These questions test a student's ability to identify and classify common objects into basic categories by one or more common physical property or attribute (e.g., color, size, shape, weight, liquid/solid, quantity, function).

- These questions test knowledge of common objects and categories, such as fruits, vegetables, flowers, reptiles, mammals, jungle animals, farm animals, tools, furniture, musical instruments, eating utensils, seasons, birds, etc.

Which picture does not belong with the others?

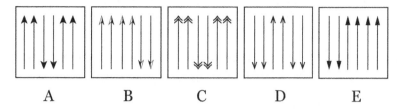

| A | B | C | D | E |

Answer: D. All pictures have four arrows pointing up and two pointing down, except D.

TIPS: Encourage your student to expand on him knowledge of a category in a question. Ask him to name other objects that share the same characteristics and belong to a specific category

Series

'Series' questions measure a student's ability to predict, according to a rule, a missing element in a series of pictures or figures.

The OLSAT® Level C can contain two types of series questions: picture series and figural series

Picture series
In picture series questions, students must examine a sequence of objects and identify/predict the object that comes next in the sequence according to the underlying pattern.

Picture series questions test students ability to identify how one or more physical property or attribute (e.g., quantity, size, weight, state (e.g.:liquid/solid), age, etc..) changes over time across the sequence.

Changes include an element or object that is added or removed, that becomes larger or smaller, increases or decreases in quantity, or becomes older or younger,etc.

SAMPLE QUESTION:

Which picture comes next?

| A | B | C | D |

Answer: C   The ice in the glass of water progressively melts. C represents the next progression.

Figural series

In figural series questions, a student must look at a sequence of geometric figures, discern a patter within the sequence, and predict the 'next' drawing/shape in the sequence.

Figural series questions test a student's ability to identify how one or more physical property or attribute (e.g., quantity, shape, size, direction, etc..) changes over time across the sequence.

Changes can include objects or elements getting bigger or smaller, increasing or decreasing in quantity, and/or combining, inverting, or rotating across rows, etc.

SAMPLE QUESTION:

Which picture comes next?

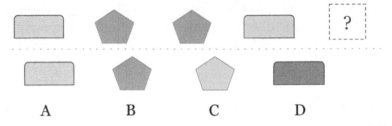

A   B   C   D

Answer: B

Pattern Matrices

"Pattern Matrix" questions, like series questions, assess a student's ability to predict, according to a rule, a missing element in a series of pictures or figures.

With this question type, a student is shown a series of figural shapes that change across the rows and columns throughout the design. These questions require the child to understand how the objects in rows and columns relate to each other. The student must isolate and apply the rule/s in order to identify which object from the answer choices fits the empty box in the bottom right-hand corner of the matrix.

SAMPLE QUESTION:

Which image best fits in the box with the question mark?

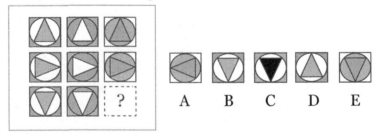

A   B   C   D   E

Answer: E

TIPS: Ask your child to explain what is happening in the matrix, and why he or she chose a specific answer. This will help you understand where your student needs support in understanding the pattern.

Encourage your student to visualize -- observe, imagine and keep track of -- the changes in the geometric shapes as they move and then draw what she predicts she might see in the empty box.

If your student is challenged with a pattern matrix question and finds it hard to detect the rule/s, take a step by step approach.

Encourage your student to discover the rule/s by looking in each direction:

- Horizontally across the rows. Ask: "How do the objects change in the first row? Do you see a pattern? Do the objects change in the same way in the second row? The third row?"
- Vertically down the columns. Ask: "How do the objects change in the first column? Do you see a pattern? Do the objects change in the same way in the second column? The third column?"
- Diagonally. Ask: "How do the objects change across the diagonal? Do you see a pattern?"

Encourage your student to isolate one element (e.g.: outer shape, inner shape/s) and identify how it changes:

- Ask: "How does the color/shading of the element change as it moves along the row/column?"
- Ask: "Does the element change positions as it moves along the row/column? Does it move up, down or around (i.e.: clockwise, counter-clockwise). Does the element move to the opposite position?"
- Ask: "Does the element get bigger, smaller or stay the same as it moves?"
- Ask: "Does the element disappear and appear again as you move along the row/column?"

OLSAT® Level C
Practice Test 1

NOTE: The 'OLSAT C' level test is most often given to a child in a one- on-one setting, with the administrator reading the question to the child. In this practice test, you can take on the role of the administrator by reading the question to your student.

Answer bubble sheets can be found at the back of the book. Please make sure your student fills in each of the bubbles fully.

1.

Which image best fits in the box with the question mark?

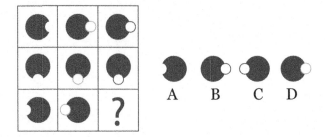

2.

Jeremy went to school with two pencils and Louis went to school with twice as many pencils. Andrew went to school with half as many pencils as Jeremy. Which picture shows the total number of pencils they brought to school?

3.

For her 7th birthday, Sophia's parents gave her 3 gifts, as you see at the beginning of the row. She got an equal number of gifts from her parents for her 6th birthday. Which picture shows how many gifts her parents gave her in total for her 6th and 7th birthdays?

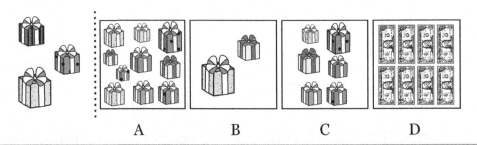

4.

Which picture comes next?

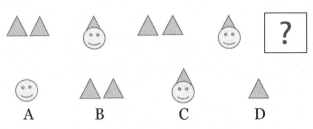

5.

Greg is wearing a black shirt, black shoes and white shorts. Jake's outfit is the opposite of Greg's. Which column of pictures shows what Jake is wearing?

A   B   C   D

6.

Which picture does not belong with the others?

A   B   C   D   E

7.

George has 8 bananas, which you see at the beginning of the row. George gave one half of his bananas to his brother. He then gave 1 banana to his sister. Which picture shows how many bananas George has left?

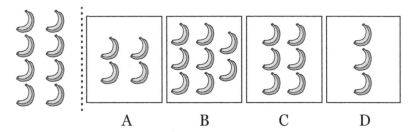

A   B   C   D

8.

Mary is planting flowers. Each plant box will have 3 flowers, as shown at the beginning of the row Which picture shows how many more more plant boxes and flowers need to be added for a total of 9 flowers?

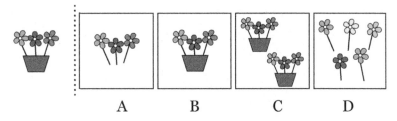

A   B   C   D

9.

Which picture comes next?

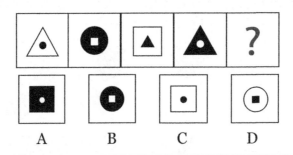

10.

Which picture shows what an architect creates?

11.

Which image best fits in the box with the question mark?

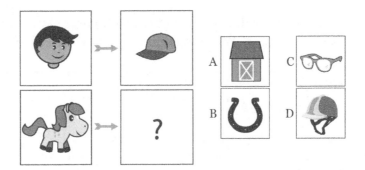

12.

In second grade, each student completes 2 worksheets of homework each day, as shown at the beginning of the row. After five days, how many total worksheets of homework has each child completed?

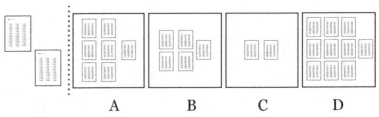

13.

Which picture does not belong with the others?

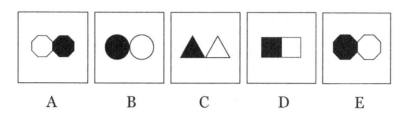

A   B   C   D   E

14.

Which column of pictures shows a square inside of a heart in between a black star and a white star?

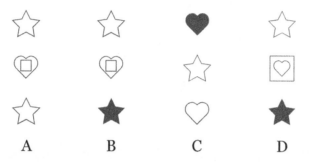

A   B   C   D

15.

Alfred's basketball team played a game last week. In the first half of the game, the team got 7 baskets, which you see at the beginning of the row. Which picture shows how many baskets the team scored in the final half of the game if they got a total of 14 baskets?

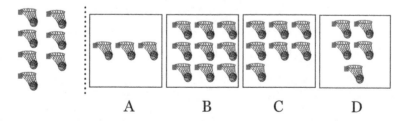

A   B   C   D

16.

Which picture does not belong with the others?

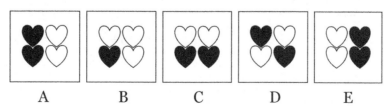

A   B   C   D   E

17.

The Brown family took a ferry to get to the island. Which picture shows the type of transportation they used?

A   B   C   D

18.

Which picture shows this: There is a black circle between a black heart and white rectangle?

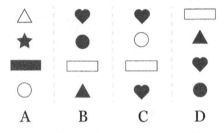

A   B   C   D

19.

Tom bought a pizza and ate 4 slices, which you see at the beginning of the row. His sister ate twice the number of slices. Which picture shows how many slices his sister ate?

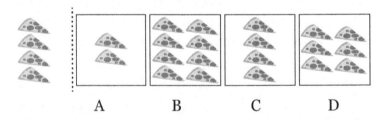

A   B   C   D

20.

Which picture does not belong with the others?

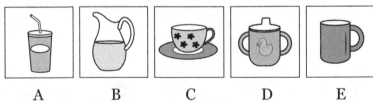

A   B   C   D   E

21.

Which picture shows this: There is a black rhombus between a black heart and white rectangle?

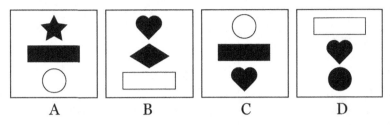

22.

Which picture does not belong with the others?

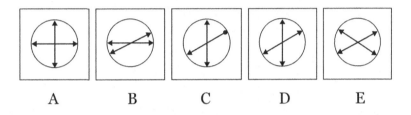

23.

Which picture comes next?

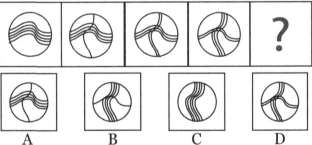

24.

Noah drew some shapes on a piece of paper. He drew a heart in the bottom right corner, a triangle in the top left corner and a star in the bottom left corner. Which picture shows what Mike drew?

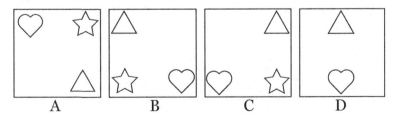

25.

Which image best fits in the box with the question mark?

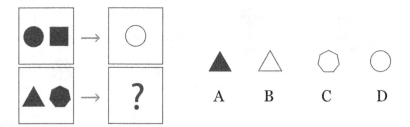

26.

Look at the numbers below. The number 1 stands for a star, and the number 3 stands for a square. Which picture shows two stars in between two squares?

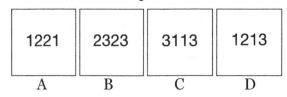

27.

Which image best fits in the box with the question mark?

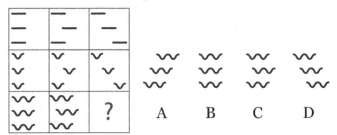

28.

Zeke has 1 angelfish and 2 guppies in his aquarium, as shown in the beginning of the row. He went to the pet shop and bought 2 more angelfish and 2 more guppies. Which picture shows how many angelfish and guppies Zeke now has?

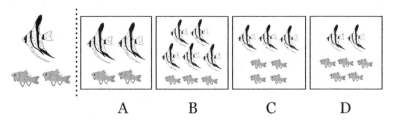

29.

Which picture does not belong with the others?

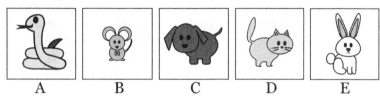

| A | B | C | D | E |

30.

Isla and Melodie both play instruments. Isla plays instruments with strings. Melodie plays the same instruments as Isla, but she also plays the flute. Which picture shows what Melodie plays?

| A | B | C | D |

31.

Arthur is playing a game with two dice. On his first turn, he rolls the number you see in the beginning of the row. On his second turn, he rolled a 6. Which picture shows what he rolled on his final 3rd turn if he scored a total of 15 with all 3 rolls?

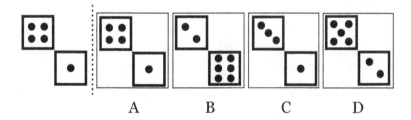

| A | B | C | D |

32.

Which image best fits in the box with the question mark?

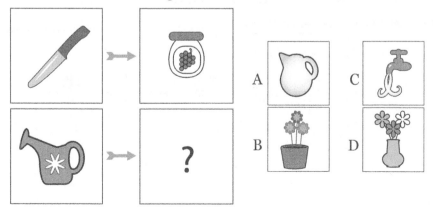

33.

Which picture does not belong with the others?

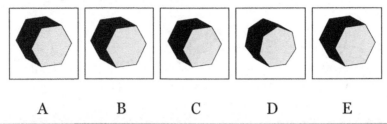

A   B   C   D   E

34.

Which image best fits in the box with the question mark?

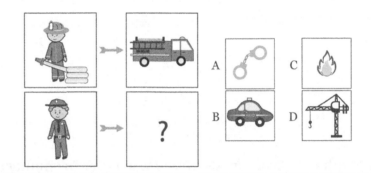

35.

Which picture does not belong with the others?

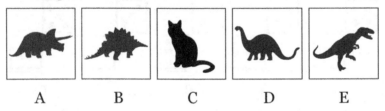

A   B   C   D   E

36.

Which image best fits in the box with the question mark?

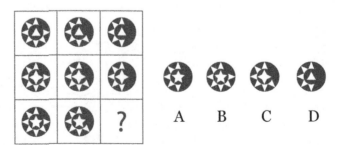

37.

Which image best fits in the box with the question mark?

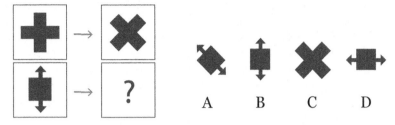

38.

Which picture does not belong with the others?

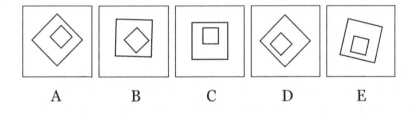

39.

Which picture does not belong with the others?

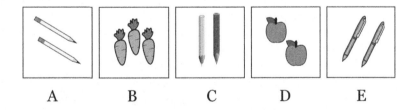

40.

Which picture comes next?

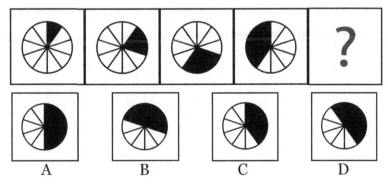

41.

Which image best fits in the box with the question mark?

 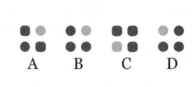

42.

Which picture does not belong with the others?

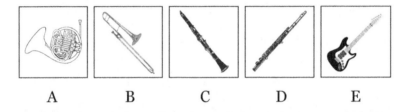

A   B   C   D   E

43.

Jerry is late for his appointment at the hospital. He wants to get to the hospital quickly. Which picture shows what he uses to get to the hospital?

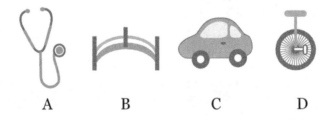

A   B   C   D

44.

Which picture does not belong with the others?

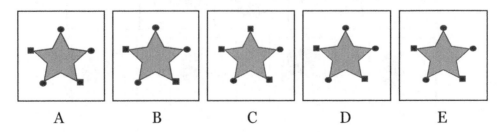

A   B   C   D   E

45.

Which image best fits in the box with the question mark?

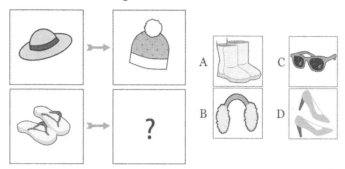

46.

Which image best fits in the box with the question mark?

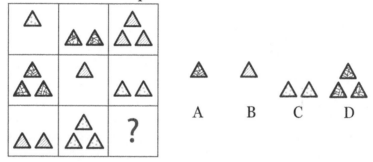

47.

Which picture comes next?

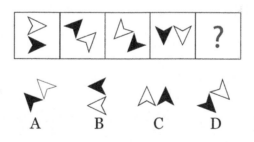

48.

Which image best fits in the box with the question mark?

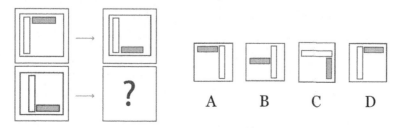

49.

Which image best fits in the box with the question mark?

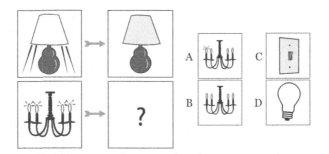

50.

Which image best fits in the box with the question mark?

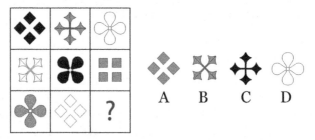

51.

To help her make dinner, Ariana used an oven, a saucepan, and a large bowl. Mark the picture which shows the kitchen equipment Ariana did not use.

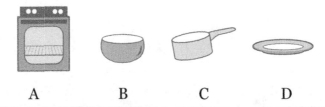

52.

Which image best fits in the box with the question mark?

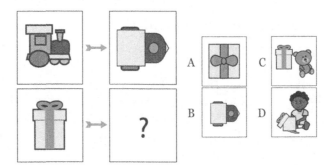

53.

Which image best fits in the box with the question mark?

54.

Which picture comes next?

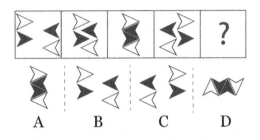

55.

Which image best fits in the box with the question mark?

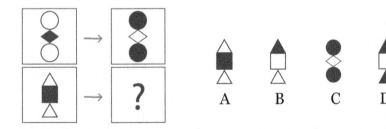

56.

Which column of pictures shows a horse below a snake, and a snake above a bee?

57.

Which image best fits in the box with the question mark?

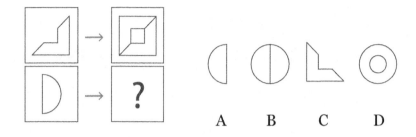

A   B   C   D

58.

Which picture comes next?

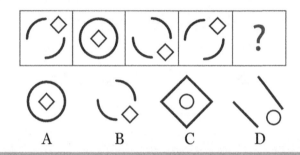

A   B   C   D

59.

Which image best fits in the box with the question mark?

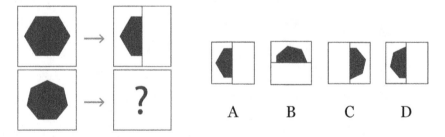

A   B   C   D

60.

Which image best fits in the box with the question mark?

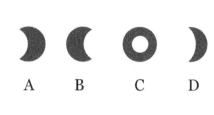

OLSAT® Level C Practice Test 2

NOTE: The 'OLSAT C' level test is most often given to a child in a one- on-one setting, with the administrator reading the question to the child. In this practice test, you can take on the role of the administrator by reading the question to your student.

Answer bubble sheets can be found at the back of the book. Please make sure your student fills in each of the bubbles fully.

1.

Which image best fits in the box with the question mark?

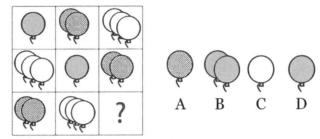

2.

Leila eats 6 strawberries every day and 2 bananas. Her sister eats half the amount of strawberries, but twice as many bananas every day. Which picture shows what Leila' sister eats every day?

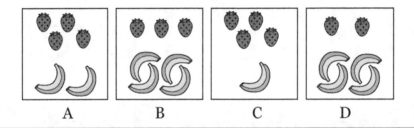

3.

Reid was looking through an astronomy book and saw a planet. Which picture shows what he saw?

4.

Which picture comes next?

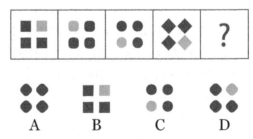

5.

Betsy is a pharmacist. Which picture shows what Betsy might use when she is working?

A   B   C   D

6.

Which picture does not belong with the others?

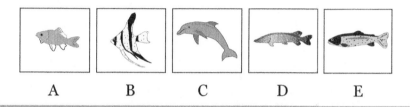

A   B   C   D   E

7.

Jackson and Isla went on vacation and saw several marine animals. Which picture shows what they saw?

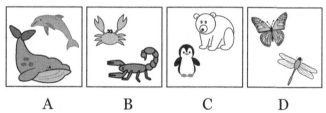

A   B   C   D

8.

Gregory bought 4 cups of lemonade from the lemonade stand, as shown in the beginning of the row. Charlotte bought an equal amount of cups of lemonade as Gregory, and Alfred bought 2 cups of lemonade. Which picture shows the total number of cups of lemonade Charlotte and Alfred bought?

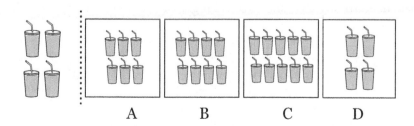

A   B   C   D

9.

Which picture comes next?

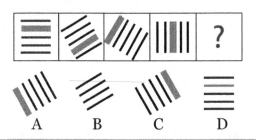

10.

Amber is measuring the perimeter of an object. Which picture shows what Amber could use to measure the perimeter?

11.

Which image best fits in the box with the question mark?

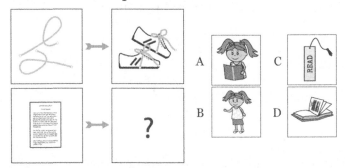

12.

Anand and 5 friends each want to buy a carton of chocolate milk. At the store, the children find a box, which contains 2 cartons of chocolate milk, as shown at the beginning of the row. Which picture shows how many more boxes the children need to buy to make sure each gets a carton of chocolate milk?

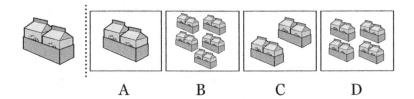

13.

Which picture does not belong with the others?

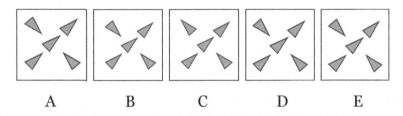

| A | B | C | D | E |

14.

Which of these items might you find in a hardware store?

| A | B | C | D |

15.

Frank already has some pairs of sneakers in his closet. Frank went shopping and bought 2 new pairs of sneakers, so now Frank has 7 pairs of sneakers, as shown at the beginning of the row. Which picture shows the number of sneakers that Frank had in his closet before he bought the new sneakers?

| A | B | C | D |

16.

Which picture does not belong with the others?

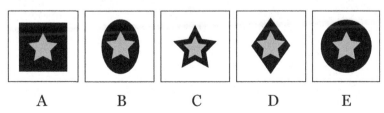

| A | B | C | D | E |

17.

Barbara is a chef. Which picture shows an item Barbara might use in her job?

A   B   C   D

18.

Which picture shows an animal that is a predator?

A   B   C   D

19.

Michael had 9 dollars, which you see at the beginning of the row. He spent 5 dollars at the grocery store, and 2 dollars at the candy store. Which picture shows how many dollars he has left?

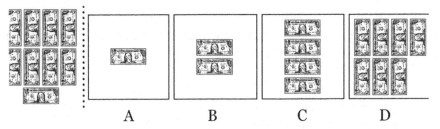

A   B   C   D

20.

Which picture does not belong with the others?

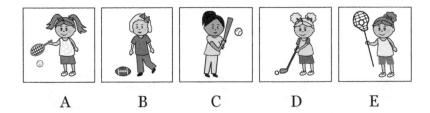

A   B   C   D   E

21.

Which picture does not belong with the others?

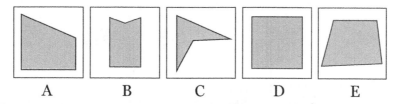

A   B   C   D   E

22.

Which picture comes next?

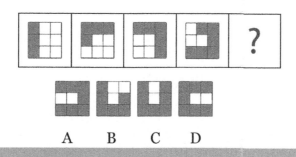

A   B   C   D

23.

Pablo is serving ice cream cones to 3 customers. Each cone has 2 scoops each, as shown at the beginning of the row. Which picture shows how many scoops total Pablo serves to his 3 customers?

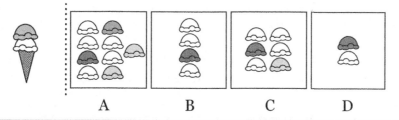

A   B   C   D

24.

Which image best fits in the box with the question mark?

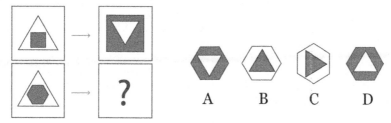

A   B   C   D

25.

Which picture shows a star below a square, and a circle above a square, with one shape shaded black?

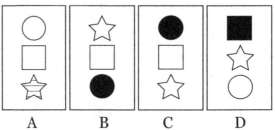

26.

Which image best fits in the box with the question mark?

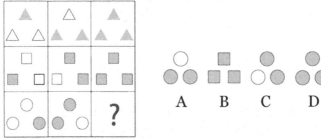

27.

Maya and her 2 friends each have a box of chocolates with 4 chocolates in it, which you see at the beginning of the row. Which picture shows the total number of chocolates that Maya and her friends have?

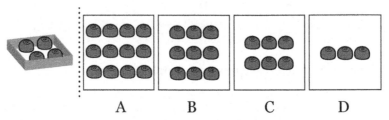

28.

Which picture does not belong with the others?

29.

Which picture shows a vacant room?

A   B   C   D

30.

Which image best fits in the box with the question mark?

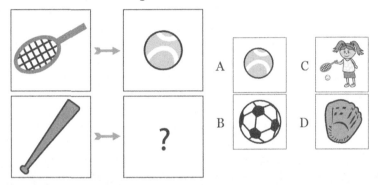

31.

Which picture does not belong with the others?

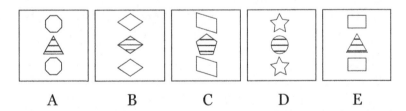

A   B   C   D   E

32.

Which picture does not belong with the others?

A   B   C   D   E

33.

Which image best fits in the box with the question mark?

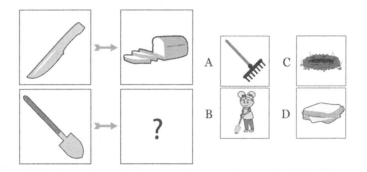

34.

Which picture shows a boy descending a steep hill?

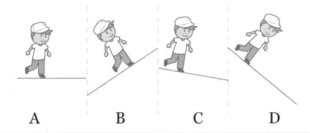

A   B   C   D

35.

Which image best fits in the box with the question mark?

A   B   C   D

36.

Which picture does not belong with the others?

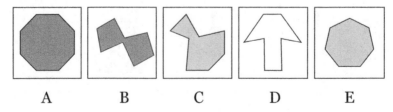

A   B   C   D   E

37.

Which picture does not belong with the others?

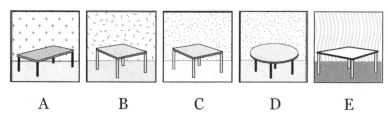

A   B   C   D   E

38.

Which picture comes next?

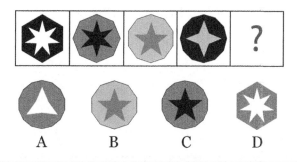

A   B   C   D

39.

Which image best fits in the box with the question mark?

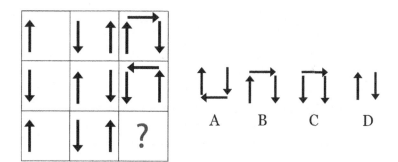

A   B   C   D

40.

Which picture does not belong with the others?

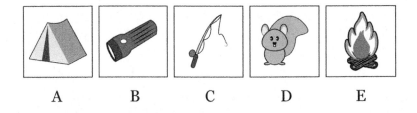

A B C D E

41.

Which picture would you choose to represent the word "vein"?

A B C D

42.

Which picture does not belong with the others?

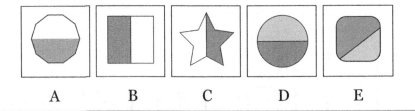

A B C D E

43.

Which image best fits in the box with the question mark?

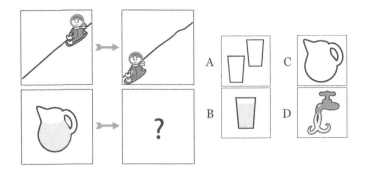

44.

Which image best fits in the box with the question mark?

 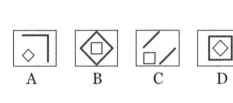

45.

Which picture comes next?

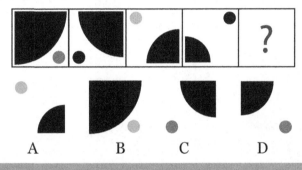

46.

Billy likes ice cream and bananas, but not broccoli or hot dogs. Ruth like hot dogs and ice cream, but not bananas or broccoli. Which picture shows the food that both Ruth and Billy dislike?

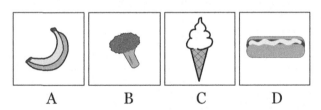

47.

Which image best fits in the box with the question mark?

48.

Which image best fits in the box with the question mark?

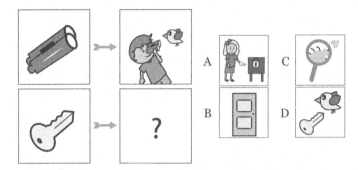

49.

Which image best fits in the box with the question mark?

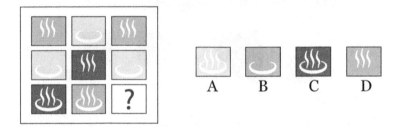

50.

Which image best fits in the box with the question mark?

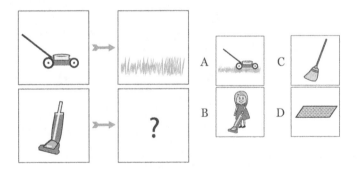

51.

Which image best fits in the box with the question mark?

 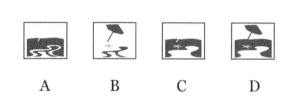

52.

Which picture comes next?

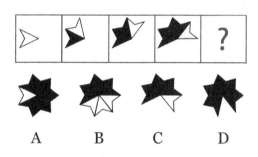

53.

In science class, Bob learned about an arid habitat. Which picture shows the habitat Bob learned about?

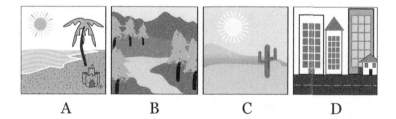

54.

Alfred went to the forest with his family. On the trail, he saw a reptile, two mammals, and an insect. Which column of pictures shows the animals that Alfred saw?

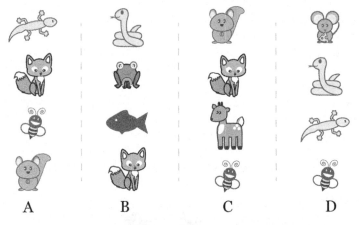

55.

Which picture comes next?

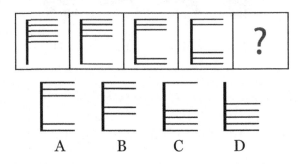

56.

Which image best fits in the box with the question mark?

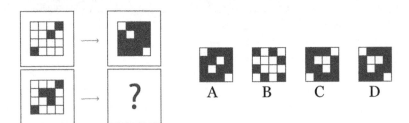

57.

Jonah went to the zoo, and saw a primate. Which picture shows what he saw?

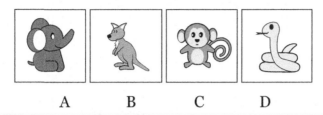

A   B   C   D

58.

Which image best fits in the box with the question mark?

59.

Which picture shows a letter between 2 numbers and a shape to the left of the number?

A   B   C   D

60.

Which image best fits in the box with the question mark?

Test One Answers

1.	C	17.	B	33.	D	49.	B
2.	D	18.	B	34.	B	50.	C
3.	C	19.	B	35.	C	51.	D
4.	B	20.	B	36.	A	52.	A
5.	D	21.	B	37.	A	53.	C
6.	E	22.	C	38.	B	54.	C
7.	D	23.	B	39.	B	55.	C
8.	C	24.	B	40.	A	56.	B
9.	D	25.	B	41.	B	57.	B
10.	C	26.	C	42.	E	58.	A
11.	B	27.	D	43.	C	59.	D
12.	D	28.	C	44.	C	60.	A
13.	A	29.	A	45.	A		
14.	B	30.	C	46.	A		
15.	C	31.	C	47.	C		
16.	B	32.	B	48.	D		

Test Two Answers

1.	D	17.	B	33.	C	49.	C
2.	B	18.	A	34.	D	50.	D
3.	A	19.	B	35.	A	51.	A
4.	D	20.	B	36.	E	52.	C
5.	A	21.	B	37.	D	53.	C
6.	C	22.	C	38.	A	54.	A
7.	A	23.	C	39.	B	55.	C
8.	A	24.	A	40.	D	56.	D
9.	C	25.	C	41.	C	57.	C
10.	B	26.	D	42.	E	58.	D
11.	D	27.	A	43.	C	59.	A
12.	C	28.	A	44.	B	60.	A
13.	C	29.	C	45.	D		
14.	C	30.	A	46.	B		
15.	A	31.	B	47.	C		
16.	C	32.	C	48.	A		

Practice Test One

> Use a No. 2 Pencil
> Fill in bubble completely.
> Ⓐ ● Ⓒ Ⓓ

Name:_____   Date:_____

1. Ⓐ Ⓑ Ⓒ Ⓓ	26. Ⓐ Ⓑ Ⓒ Ⓓ	51. Ⓐ Ⓑ Ⓒ Ⓓ
2. Ⓐ Ⓑ Ⓒ Ⓓ	27. Ⓐ Ⓑ Ⓒ Ⓓ	52. Ⓐ Ⓑ Ⓒ Ⓓ
3. Ⓐ Ⓑ Ⓒ Ⓓ	28. Ⓐ Ⓑ Ⓒ Ⓓ	53. Ⓐ Ⓑ Ⓒ Ⓓ
4. Ⓐ Ⓑ Ⓒ Ⓓ	29. Ⓐ Ⓑ Ⓒ Ⓓ Ⓔ	54. Ⓐ Ⓑ Ⓒ Ⓓ
5. Ⓐ Ⓑ Ⓒ Ⓓ	30. Ⓐ Ⓑ Ⓒ Ⓓ	55. Ⓐ Ⓑ Ⓒ Ⓓ
6. Ⓐ Ⓑ Ⓒ Ⓓ Ⓔ	31. Ⓐ Ⓑ Ⓒ Ⓓ	56. Ⓐ Ⓑ Ⓒ Ⓓ
7. Ⓐ Ⓑ Ⓒ Ⓓ	32. Ⓐ Ⓑ Ⓒ Ⓓ	57. Ⓐ Ⓑ Ⓒ Ⓓ
8. Ⓐ Ⓑ Ⓒ Ⓓ	33. Ⓐ Ⓑ Ⓒ Ⓓ Ⓔ	58. Ⓐ Ⓑ Ⓒ Ⓓ
9. Ⓐ Ⓑ Ⓒ Ⓓ	34. Ⓐ Ⓑ Ⓒ Ⓓ	59. Ⓐ Ⓑ Ⓒ Ⓓ
10. Ⓐ Ⓑ Ⓒ Ⓓ	35. Ⓐ Ⓑ Ⓒ Ⓓ Ⓔ	60. Ⓐ Ⓑ Ⓒ Ⓓ
11. Ⓐ Ⓑ Ⓒ Ⓓ	36. Ⓐ Ⓑ Ⓒ Ⓓ	
12. Ⓐ Ⓑ Ⓒ Ⓓ	37. Ⓐ Ⓑ Ⓒ Ⓓ	
13. Ⓐ Ⓑ Ⓒ Ⓓ Ⓔ	38. Ⓐ Ⓑ Ⓒ Ⓓ Ⓔ	
14. Ⓐ Ⓑ Ⓒ Ⓓ	39. Ⓐ Ⓑ Ⓒ Ⓓ Ⓔ	
15. Ⓐ Ⓑ Ⓒ Ⓓ	40. Ⓐ Ⓑ Ⓒ Ⓓ	
16. Ⓐ Ⓑ Ⓒ Ⓓ Ⓔ	41. Ⓐ Ⓑ Ⓒ Ⓓ	
17. Ⓐ Ⓑ Ⓒ Ⓓ	42. Ⓐ Ⓑ Ⓒ Ⓓ Ⓔ	
18. Ⓐ Ⓑ Ⓒ Ⓓ	43. Ⓐ Ⓑ Ⓒ Ⓓ	
19. Ⓐ Ⓑ Ⓒ Ⓓ	44. Ⓐ Ⓑ Ⓒ Ⓓ Ⓔ	
20. Ⓐ Ⓑ Ⓒ Ⓓ Ⓔ	45. Ⓐ Ⓑ Ⓒ Ⓓ	
21. Ⓐ Ⓑ Ⓒ Ⓓ	46. Ⓐ Ⓑ Ⓒ Ⓓ	
22. Ⓐ Ⓑ Ⓒ Ⓓ Ⓔ	47. Ⓐ Ⓑ Ⓒ Ⓓ	
23. Ⓐ Ⓑ Ⓒ Ⓓ	48. Ⓐ Ⓑ Ⓒ Ⓓ	
24. Ⓐ Ⓑ Ⓒ Ⓓ	49. Ⓐ Ⓑ Ⓒ Ⓓ	
25. Ⓐ Ⓑ Ⓒ Ⓓ	50. Ⓐ Ⓑ Ⓒ Ⓓ	

Practice Test Two

Use a No. 2 Pencil
Fill in bubble completely.

Ⓐ ● Ⓒ Ⓓ

Name:_____   Date:_____

1. Ⓐ Ⓑ Ⓒ Ⓓ
2. Ⓐ Ⓑ Ⓒ Ⓓ
3. Ⓐ Ⓑ Ⓒ Ⓓ
4. Ⓐ Ⓑ Ⓒ Ⓓ
5. Ⓐ Ⓑ Ⓒ Ⓓ
6. Ⓐ Ⓑ Ⓒ Ⓓ Ⓔ
7. Ⓐ Ⓑ Ⓒ Ⓓ
8. Ⓐ Ⓑ Ⓒ Ⓓ
9. Ⓐ Ⓑ Ⓒ Ⓓ
10. Ⓐ Ⓑ Ⓒ Ⓓ
11. Ⓐ Ⓑ Ⓒ Ⓓ
12. Ⓐ Ⓑ Ⓒ Ⓓ
13. Ⓐ Ⓑ Ⓒ Ⓓ Ⓔ
14. Ⓐ Ⓑ Ⓒ Ⓓ
15. Ⓐ Ⓑ Ⓒ Ⓓ
16. Ⓐ Ⓑ Ⓒ Ⓓ Ⓔ
17. Ⓐ Ⓑ Ⓒ Ⓓ
18. Ⓐ Ⓑ Ⓒ Ⓓ
19. Ⓐ Ⓑ Ⓒ Ⓓ
20. Ⓐ Ⓑ Ⓒ Ⓓ Ⓔ
21. Ⓐ Ⓑ Ⓒ Ⓓ Ⓔ
22. Ⓐ Ⓑ Ⓒ Ⓓ
23. Ⓐ Ⓑ Ⓒ Ⓓ
24. Ⓐ Ⓑ Ⓒ Ⓓ
25. Ⓐ Ⓑ Ⓒ Ⓓ

26. Ⓐ Ⓑ Ⓒ Ⓓ
27. Ⓐ Ⓑ Ⓒ Ⓓ
28. Ⓐ Ⓑ Ⓒ Ⓓ Ⓔ
29. Ⓐ Ⓑ Ⓒ Ⓓ
30. Ⓐ Ⓑ Ⓒ Ⓓ
31. Ⓐ Ⓑ Ⓒ Ⓓ Ⓔ
32. Ⓐ Ⓑ Ⓒ Ⓓ Ⓔ
33. Ⓐ Ⓑ Ⓒ Ⓓ
34. Ⓐ Ⓑ Ⓒ Ⓓ
35. Ⓐ Ⓑ Ⓒ Ⓓ
36. Ⓐ Ⓑ Ⓒ Ⓓ Ⓔ
37. Ⓐ Ⓑ Ⓒ Ⓓ Ⓔ
38. Ⓐ Ⓑ Ⓒ Ⓓ
39. Ⓐ Ⓑ Ⓒ Ⓓ
40. Ⓐ Ⓑ Ⓒ Ⓓ Ⓔ
41. Ⓐ Ⓑ Ⓒ Ⓓ
42. Ⓐ Ⓑ Ⓒ Ⓓ Ⓔ
43. Ⓐ Ⓑ Ⓒ Ⓓ
44. Ⓐ Ⓑ Ⓒ Ⓓ
45. Ⓐ Ⓑ Ⓒ Ⓓ
46. Ⓐ Ⓑ Ⓒ Ⓓ
47. Ⓐ Ⓑ Ⓒ Ⓓ
48. Ⓐ Ⓑ Ⓒ Ⓓ
49. Ⓐ Ⓑ Ⓒ Ⓓ
50. Ⓐ Ⓑ Ⓒ Ⓓ

51. Ⓐ Ⓑ Ⓒ Ⓓ
52. Ⓐ Ⓑ Ⓒ Ⓓ
53. Ⓐ Ⓑ Ⓒ Ⓓ
54. Ⓐ Ⓑ Ⓒ Ⓓ
55. Ⓐ Ⓑ Ⓒ Ⓓ
56. Ⓐ Ⓑ Ⓒ Ⓓ
57. Ⓐ Ⓑ Ⓒ Ⓓ
58. Ⓐ Ⓑ Ⓒ Ⓓ
59. Ⓐ Ⓑ Ⓒ Ⓓ
60. Ⓐ Ⓑ Ⓒ Ⓓ

Answer Explanations

Test One:

1. C. Pattern matrix. Across the rows, the outline of the smaller circles grows darker. Down the columns, the smaller circle rotates clockwise around the edge of the larger circle.

2. D. Following directions.

3. C. Arithmetic reasoning.

4. B. Series. Shapes alternate.

5. D. Aural reasoning.

6. E. Classification: Objects connected to a day a the beach, except E.

7. D. Arithmetic reasoning.

8. C. Arithmetic reasoning.

9. D. Series. In each frame, there are two shapes. The inner shape forms the outer shape of the next frame. Hence choices A and C can be eliminated. Alternate outer shapes are shaded. Hence choice D that has no shaded/white outer shape is the correct answer.

10. C. Aural reasoning.

11. B. Analogy: A boy wears a cap like a horse wears a horseshoe.

12. D. Arithmetic reasoning.

13. A. Classification. Black shape followed b white shape, except A.

14. B. Following directions.

15. C. Arithmetic reasoning.

16. B. Classification. Two black and two whit hearts, except B.

17. B. Aural Reasoning.

18. B. Following directions.

19. B. Arithmetic reasoning.

20. B. Classification. Types of cups

21. B. Aural reasoning.

22. C. Classification. A circle which contains tw lines with arrowheads at either end of the lines.

23. B. Series. In the first frame there are horizontal loops. In each frame, horizontal loop decreases by one and vertical loop increases by one. Hence choice B that has 1 horizontal loop and 4 vertical loops is the correct answer.

24. B. Following directions.

25. B. Analogy.

26. C. Aural Reasoning.

27. D. Pattern matrix. Across the rows, the middle and bottom shapes move toward the opposite edge. Down the columns, the shape/line becomes distorted.

28. C. Arithmetic reasoning.

29. A. Classification. Mammals

30. C. Aural reasoning.

31. C. Arithmetic reasoning.

32. B. Analogy. A knife is used to spread jelly as a watering can is used to water a plant.

33. D. Classification. Hexagons.

34. B. Analogy. A fireman drives a fire engine li a policeman drives in a police car.

35. C. Classification. Silhouettes of dinosaur

36. A. Pattern matrix. Across the rows, the number of points on the outer star decrease by one. Down the columns, the points on the inner star increase by one.

37. A. Analogy. Image turns quarter turn

counterclockwise.

38. B. Classification. Side of inside small squar is parallel to side of outside larger square

39. B. Classification. Two items

40. A. Series. In each frame, an additional portion is shaded. Hence choice C can be eliminated. An additional portion is added to the right side of the shaded portion in the previous frame. Also the shaded portion begins at a place where the shaded portion of the previous frame ends. Hence choice A is the correct answer.

41. B. Pattern matrix. Across the rows, the group of shapes rotate counterclockwise. Down the columns, the group of shapes rotate counterclockwise while the shapes within the group become more round.

42. E. Classification. Wind instruments

43. C. Aural reasoning.

44. C. Classification. Two squares and thre circles at the end of the star's points.

45. A. Analogy. A summer hat is to a winter hat like summer shoes are to winter shoes.

46. A. Pattern matrix. Both across and down, the triangles alternate between groups of 1, 2 and 3 triangles and between 3 patterns.

47. C. Series. As the pair of arrows progress from left to right, they rotate counter-clockwise 45 degrees and 180 degrees, and swap color with each 45 degree rotation.

48. D. Analogy. Inside shapes flip 180 degrees

49. B. Analogy. Lights turn off

50. C. Pattern matrix. In the matrix, from left to right, you see that the figures change across the row. The shade of each figure also changes across the rows. Down the columns, the figures likewise change shape and shade but also rotate 45 degrees.

51. D. Following directions.

52. A. Analogy. View of item from side and then from top.

53. C. Pattern matrix. Across, the outermost circle alternates between black, medium gray and light gray while the innermost circle alternates between black and medium gray. Down, the center circle (white) expands while the innermost circle alternates between black and medium gray.

54. C. Series. Each group of arrows move past one another.

55. D. Analogy. Shapes switch colors.

56. B. Following directions.

57. B. Analogy. Second mirror shape is added.

58. A. Series. The line segments alternate back and forth to form a complete circle every third cycle while the diamond alternates with the line segments but moves to the center every third cycle when the circle is completed.

59. D. Analogy. Shape is split in half so only left side shows.

60. A. Pattern matrix. Across, the small circle moves past the larger circle. Down, the smaller circle increases in size.

Test Two:

1. D. Pattern matrix. Across the rows and down the columns, the objects alternate between one gray balloon, two black balloons and three white balloons.

2. B. Aural reasoning.

3. A. Aural reasoning.

4. D. Series. The group of squares rotates counterclockwise across the row as the squares become circles then revert once more to their

original shape but at 45 degrees.

5. A. Aural reasoning.

6.C. Classification. Types of fis

7. A. Aural reasoning.

8.A. Arithmetic reasoning.

9. C. Series. The group of lines rotate counterclockwise 30 degrees across the row while the gray thick line moves two lines (in the direction of the towards bottom line and then back to top again) with each rotation.

10.   B. Aural reasoning.

11. D. Analogy. Shoelaces are part of sneakers like pages a part of a book.

12. C. Arithmetic reasoning.

13. C. Classification. Three arrows poin diagonally from bottom left to top right. Two arrows point inwards from the top left and bottom right corners.

14.C. Aural reasoning.

15. A. Arithmetic reasoning.

16. C. Classification. A gray star inside different black shape

17. B. Aural reasoning.

18. A. Aural reasoning.

19. B. Arithmetic reasoning.

20.B. Classification. Games played with bat club/racquet etc. and ball.

21. B. Classification. Four sided shapes

22. C. Series. The pattern begins by displaying a cube sectioned into nine equal parts. The firs column, containing three of the nine sections, is colored and the rest are left white. As the pattern progresses, the cube rotates to the right

shifting the colored section from the far left, to the top row of the cube. Following this rotating pattern, the correct choice can only be answer option 'D' or 'B'. The pattern also depicts one additional section of the cube being shaded in as each sequence progresses. By counting the shaded boxes in each image, it can be deduced that the final image must have seven sections in color, leaving answer option 'C' as the only viable answer.

23. C. Arithmetic reasoning.

24. A. Analogy. The outside shape becomes the inside shape and turns upside down.

25. C. Following directions.

26. D. Pattern matrix.

27. A. Arithmetic reasoning.

28. A. Classification. Farm animal

29. C. Aural reasoning.

30. A. Analogy. A tennis racquet is used to hit a tennis ball like a baseball bat is used to hit a baseball.

31. B. Classification. Three shapes in a vertica column. The shape in the middle is differen from the shapes on the top and bottom, which are the same.

32. C. Classification. Water sports

33. C. Analogy. A knife is used as a tool to cut bread like a shovel is used as a tool to dig earth.

34. D. Following directions.

35. A. Analogy. The inside shapes flip 18 degrees.

36. E. Classification. Eight sided figure

37. D. Classification. Four sided tables

38. A. Series. The outer geometric shape adds one point (two sides) while the inner star deletes

one point (two sides) and both inner and outer shapes alternate in shade.

39. B. Pattern matrix.

40. D. Classification. Items used while camping

41. C. Aural reasoning.

42. E. Classification. Shapes half shaded

43. C. Analogy. Top to bottom/ High to low.

44. B. Pattern matrix. The shapes combine down each column to form the bottom element while the shapes alternate across the columns.

45. D. Series. The quarter moon and circle rotate clockwise while the quarter moon gradually shrinks and grows and the circle alternates between two shades of gray and black.

46. B. Following directions.

47. C. Analogy. Three shapes on a diagonal. Top and bottom shapes swap colors, while three shapes retain same diagonal direction.

48. A. Analogy. Binoculars can be used by a person to see a bird up close; a key can be used by a person to open a safe.

49. C. Pattern matrix. The shapes alternate across and down the top two columns and combine in the third row to complete the graphic while the background colors alternate throughout the matrix.

50. D. Analogy. A mower mows grass; a vacuum vacuums carpets.

51. A. Pattern matrix. The shapes combine from bottom to top and from left to right to form the final scene in the top right corner

52. C. Series. Starts with one white arrow, which moves clockwise throughout sequence. Each sequence adds an additional black arrow in a counter clockwise direction.

53. C. Aural reasoning.

54. A. Following directions.

55. C. Series. In the pattern displayed, a vertical post supports five horizontal lines. Each tim the pattern progresses, the lowest horizontal line is moved to the lowest position available on the vertical post. By counting the progression of the lines in the pattern, the answer should show a total of four lines resting at the bottom of the vertical post. Thus the correct answer can only be option C.

56. D. Analogy. Outer square turns ¼ turn anticlockwise and inner cubes swap colors.

57. C. Aural reasoning.

58. D. Pattern matrix. The color/shade of the outer ring alternates across the row but stays the same down each column. Across the row, the number and/or position of black diamonds change. Down the column, the black diamonds change position.

59. A. Following directions.

60. A. Pattern matrix. The background color/ shade and polygon alternate across and down.